Journal for Women

Copyright © 2014

All rights reserved. No part of this publication may be reproduced, distributed or transmitted in any form or by any means, including photocopying, recording, or other electronic or mechanical methods, without the prior written permission of the publisher, except in the case of brief quotations embodied in critical reviews and certain other noncommercial uses permitted by copyright law. For permission requests, write to the publisher, addressed "Attention: Permissions Coordinator," at the address below.

Speedy Publishing LLC
40 E. Main St., #1156,
Newark, DE 19711
www.speedypublishing.co

Publisher's Note: This is a work of fiction. Names, characters, places, and incidents are a product of the author's imagination. Locales and public names are sometimes used for atmospheric purposes. Any resemblance to actual people, living or dead, or to businesses, companies, events, institutions, or locales is completely coincidental.

Speedy Publishing LLC©2014

Ordering Information:
Quantity sales. Special discounts are available on quantity purchases by corporations, associations, and others. For details, contact the "Special Sales Department" at the address above.

Journal for Women -- 1st ed.
ISBN 978-1-6328795-4-7

Date _______________________

Date _______________________

Date ___________________

Date _______________________

Date ________________________

Date ___________________

Date _______________________

Date _________________________

Date _______________________

Date ___________________

Date ___________________

Date _______________________

Date _______________________

Date _______________________

Date _______________________

Date _______________________

Date ______________________

Date _________________________

Date _______________________

Date ________________________

Date _________________________

Date _________________________

Date _______________________

Date _______________________

Date _____________________

Date _________________

Date ___________________

Date _______________________

Date _____________________

Date _______________________

Date _____________________

Date _______________________

Date _______________________

Date ___________________

Date ___________________

Date ______________________

Date ________________

Date _______________________

Date ______________________

Date ________________________

Date _________________________

Date _____________________

Date ________________________

Date _______________________

Date _______________________

Date ______________________

Date _______________________

Date _________________